PLANET EARTH PROJECTS

Oksana Kemarskaya

DOVER PUBLICATIONS, INC.
Mineola, New York

Before starting any of these projects, please let an adult know so they can supervise. Many of the projects in this book require help from an adult. This is indicated by a caution symbol located at the top of the page.

Bibliographical Note

Planet Earth Projects is a new work, first published by
Dover Publications, Inc., in 2011.

International Standard Book Number

ISBN-13: 978-0-486-47923-1
ISBN-10: 0-486-47923-4

Manufactured in the United States by Courier Corporation
47923401
www.doverpublications.com

Contents

Garbage Chart

Scientists use charts to keep track of information. These records can be very useful. Make a chart to record how many garbage bags you throw out each week.

1. Write "Garbage Chart" across the top of a piece of paper. Then draw a line near the bottom and near the left side of the paper.

2. Next to the line at the left (near the page edge) number 0 through 20 starting with 0 at the bottom and ending with 20 at the top.

3. At the bottom of the paper (near the page edge) write Week 1, Week 2, Week 3, and Week 4.

4. Each week make an X on the chart to keep track of how many garbage bags are thrown out. Now that you have this information, try and recycle more so you throw out less garbage bags every week.

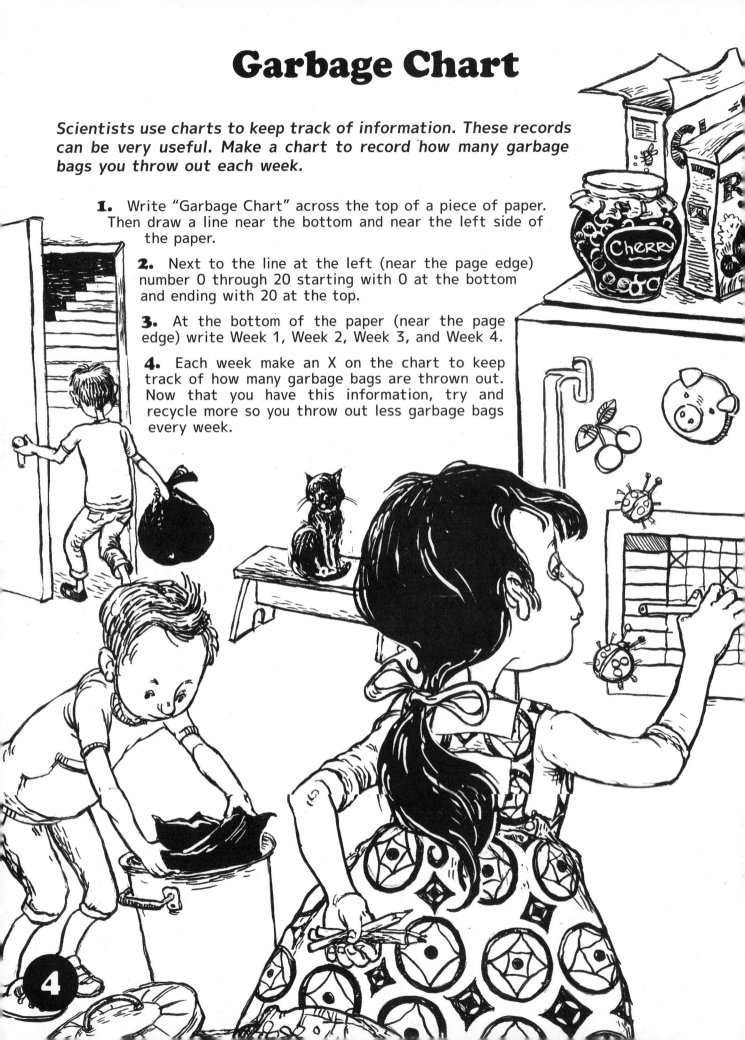

Paper

Did you know that factories recycle old paper to make new paper? Recycled paper helps keep trees alive. This is important because trees help filter the air we breathe. You can recycle paper, too!

1. Take 2 or 3 sheets of used paper and tear them into pieces. Place the pieces into a blender.

2. Ask an adult to help you with the blender. Add water into the blender until the mixture is very watery, this is called a slurry.

3. Place a screen between two open picture frames. The screen will hold the paper and the frames will shape it into a square.

4. Hold the frame over a sink and pour the slurry onto the screen so the water can drain from the mixture.

5. Let the paper dry for at least 24 hours. When it's dry, you can use it to write or draw whatever you want.

Recycled Crayons

1. Gather all of your old, broken crayons.

2. Remove the paper from the crayons.

3. Sort the crayon pieces into piles of the same color.

4. Ask an adult to help you chop the crayon pieces into small bits.

5. Get a mini muffin tin and place waxed paper liners in each of the cups. Fill each cup halfway with crayon bits of different colors.

6. Have an adult place the tin in a 250 degree oven until the crayons are melted. Remove the tin from the oven and let it cool for at least one hour.

7. Carefully peel off the paper from your new crayons and start coloring!

6

Herb Garden

Fresh herbs like basil, rosemary, thyme, oregano, sage, and mint, can be grown inside any month of the year. They are good to use in cooking and they smell nice, hang them to dry and they will last a long time.

1. Fill a clay pot or recycled container with good soil.

2. Sprinkle on some herb seeds.

3. Add some more soil on top.

4. Water it when you first plant the seeds and whenever the earth gets dry.

Paper Boat

People during the Stone Age made boats out of wood and animal skins. The first trip around the world was by boat. Make your own paper boat by following these simple instructions.

1. Follow the instructions on the right to fold a boat out of one sheet of paper.

2. Launch your boat in the water. For more fun, try racing your boat against other paper boats.

Paper Airplane

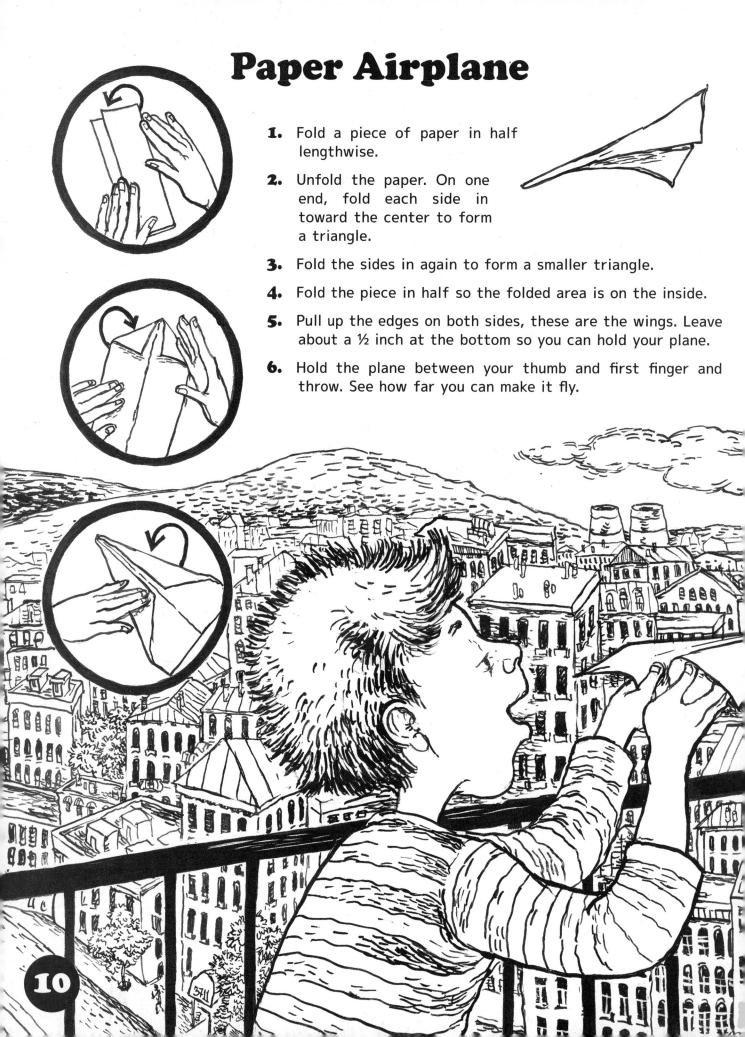

1. Fold a piece of paper in half lengthwise.

2. Unfold the paper. On one end, fold each side in toward the center to form a triangle.

3. Fold the sides in again to form a smaller triangle.

4. Fold the piece in half so the folded area is on the inside.

5. Pull up the edges on both sides, these are the wings. Leave about a ½ inch at the bottom so you can hold your plane.

6. Hold the plane between your thumb and first finger and throw. See how far you can make it fly.

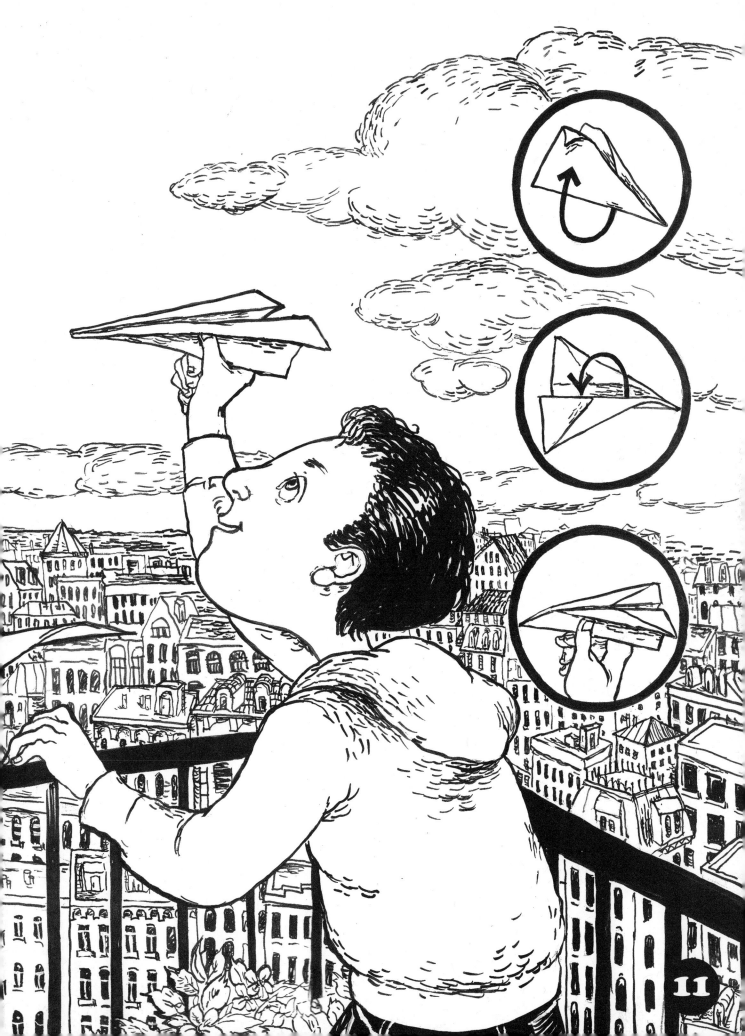

Onions

Onions need a lot of green top growth in order for the bulb to form. The tops send energy down to the bulb so the onion can grow. When you eat the green top from an onion you are actually eating stored energy.

1. Find an onion that is already starting to sprout from the top.

2. Put the bottom part with the roots into a jar of water. (Be careful not to put the onion part in the water or else it will rot.) Place the jar in a spot where it gets medium sunlight.

3. The onion tops and roots should start growing in a few weeks. When the tops are big carefully cut them off (not all the way) using scissors. Enjoy them sprinkled on a salad or use them in a favorite recipe.

Sunflowers

Sunflowers can grow 8 to 12 feet high in just 6 months. The largest sunflower on record was almost 25½ feet tall!

1. Plant 3 unroasted sunflower seeds in a pot indoors. You can also plant the seeds right outside in the ground. Plant them a foot apart and make sure to choose a spot that is sunny and not too windy.

2. When your indoor plants start to get too big, then it's time to plant them outside. Follow the planting instructions in #1.

3. Put a tall stick into the ground next to the sunflower plant and gently tie the stem (not too tight) to the stick. This will help the sunflower stay up.

4. Remember to water your sunflower!

Can Planter

Many things can be recycled into planters. Plastic containers, milk cartons, buckets, old pots, and plastic egg cartons are all good to save and use for planting. Here is how to make a tin can into a planter.

1. Wash a tin can and remove the label.

2. Ask an adult to put a few nail holes in the bottom of the can for drainage. You can use an old lid to put underneath the can to catch the extra water.

3. Make your own label for the can out of paper and glue it in place. You can write what type of plant you are growing, or just give it a name.

4. Fill the can with soil and put a plant in it or a few seeds.

5. Water your plant and put it where it will get some sunlight.

Organic Air Freshener

1. Find a nice plump orange and some cloves. Stick the cloves into the orange.

2. Put the orange on a shelf or hang it from a string.

3. Tying a ribbon around your natural air freshener will make it even prettier.

An orange is a fruit that grows on small flowering trees. A group of orange trees is called an orange grove. Cloves are also from a tree. They are dried flower buds that are used as a spice. When your natural air freshener no longer has a scent, you can put it into a compost pile so it can decompose and turn back into soil.

Natural Lemonade

1. Have an adult help you make simple syrup by mixing ¼ cup of sugar with ¼ cup of hot water. Mix it until it is all dissolved.

2. Squeeze the juice from 4 whole lemons over a strainer (to catch the seeds) into a cup.

3. Add the lemon juice and simple syrup to a pitcher of fresh cold water.

4. After you mix it all up, pour yourself a cup and add some ice. Natural lemonade is better for you and for the planet because it has no packaging waste. It tastes better, too!

Lemonade Stand

Selling natural lemonade is a way to share a healthy drink with people, and a way to make some money. Choose a hot day and get out there and start selling!

1. You will need a good amount of fresh natural lemonade, cups, and ice.

2. Make a sign that says "Real Lemonade" and the amount it will cost for a cup.

3. Have a box handy for the money. Start your day off with some change in the box in case customers don't have the exact amount you are charging.

Almond Milk

Nuts and seeds have natural oils and nutrients in them that help make us strong and healthy.

1. Have an adult put 2 handfuls of almonds in a blender with 1 date (without the pit) and 1½ cups of water. Blend for a couple of seconds.

2. Pour on top of granola and eat.

Granola

Eating fresh whole foods is good for you because they have more nutrients than packaged foods and contain no preservatives. It is also good for the environment because there is no packaging to throw out. Granola is a natural food that is good for breakfast or a snack.

1. Take 2 cups of dried oats, a ½ cup of seeds without the shells (sunflower, pumpkin, or any other type of seeds), ½ cup of dried fruit like raisins, and soak all the ingredients in a bowl of water overnight. Drain the water.

2. Have an adult put everything in a food processor and mix it for a couple of seconds so it is chunky but chopped up.

3. Add a pinch of cinnamon or nutmeg and a small pinch of salt.

4. Place your granola in the bottom of the prepared baking pan and bake for 30 minutes.

5. Put some fresh berries or sliced fruit on top and enjoy!

Roots

Plants get the nutrients they need from the soil through their roots. Did you know that you can grow a new houseplant with just a leaf clipping?

1. Have an adult cut a leaf from a houseplant using scissors (make sure to leave part of the stem).

2. Place the stem of the leaf in a small bottle filled with water.

3. When you see long, healthy roots then your new houseplant is ready to be planted in soil.

Carrot Top

The green leafy top of a carrot that is normally thrown out in the garbage can actually grow a new plant. You won't make new carrots, but you will have a nice new plant. You can also try this with a pineapple top.

1. Find an old yogurt or margarine container and fill it with some soil.

2. Take your carrot top and plant it in the soil so only the green leaves are showing.

3. Water your plant and watch it grow!

Sprouts

1. You can find sprout seeds in health food stores. Put 2 tablespoons of the seeds in a jar and cover them with water.

2. Put 2 or 3 layers of cheesecloth over the top of the jar. Tie the cheesecloth onto the jar with string or use a rubber band to keep it in place.

3. Soak the seeds in water for 24 hours.

4. Turn the jar upside down to drain the water. Add some water to the jar to rinse them and drain off excess water.

5. Rinse your seeds every 12 hours to keep them wet and clean. When you see small green leaves they will be ready to eat.

Broom

1. Break small sticks off a fallen branch or find some small twigs on the ground. Remove all of the leaves off the twigs.

2. Find a long stick. This will be your broom handle. Grab a handful of the small sticks and tie them on one end of the long stick using a vine or some string.

3. Push some more small twigs into the bundle until the vine or string is tight and start sweeping!

Kite

Decorate your kite any way you want, but use bright colors so you will be able to see it high in the sky.

1. You will need a large piece of strong paper. Take a ruler and draw a diamond shape from edge to edge on the paper. Measure 2 inches in from the edge of the diamond and draw another diamond. Draw your design inside the diamond.

2. Have an adult cut 2 sticks or wooden dowels for you. One stick should be long enough to go from top to the bottom of your kite; the other one should go from side to side. Cut a small notch in each end of the sticks.

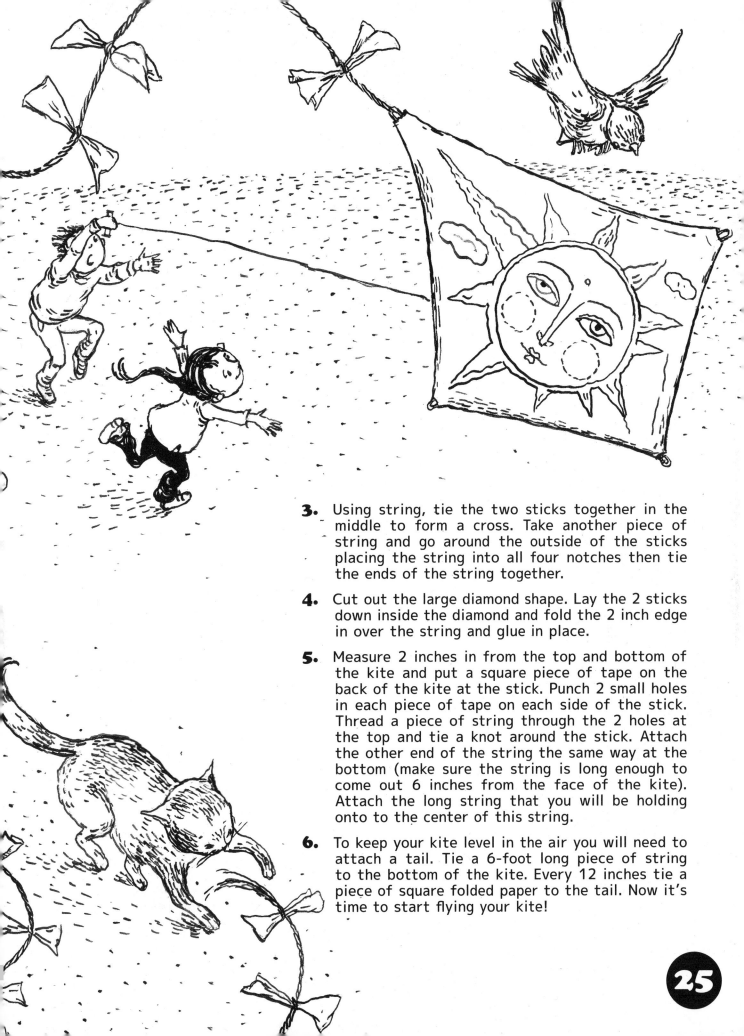

3. Using string, tie the two sticks together in the middle to form a cross. Take another piece of string and go around the outside of the sticks placing the string into all four notches then tie the ends of the string together.

4. Cut out the large diamond shape. Lay the 2 sticks down inside the diamond and fold the 2 inch edge in over the string and glue in place.

5. Measure 2 inches in from the top and bottom of the kite and put a square piece of tape on the back of the kite at the stick. Punch 2 small holes in each piece of tape on each side of the stick. Thread a piece of string through the 2 holes at the top and tie a knot around the stick. Attach the other end of the string the same way at the bottom (make sure the string is long enough to come out 6 inches from the face of the kite). Attach the long string that you will be holding onto to the center of this string.

6. To keep your kite level in the air you will need to attach a tail. Tie a 6-foot long piece of string to the bottom of the kite. Every 12 inches tie a piece of square folded paper to the tail. Now it's time to start flying your kite!

Wind Powered Pinwheel

Wind is a source of renewable energy, which means it comes from a natural resource that is always replenished. Wind turbines convert energy into electricity. A pinwheel is powered by air just like a wind turbine. Here's how to make your own pinwheel using a piece of paper, a pencil, and a pushpin.

1. Fold a square piece of paper in half from corner to corner, unfold, and fold the other part in half from corner to corner and unfold.

2. Using scissors, carefully cut along the folded lines almost to the center.

3. Take one corner from each piece and pull it toward the center.

4. Stick a pushpin through the center of your pinwheel then into the side of a pencil eraser. Hold the pinwheel up into the wind and watch it spin!

Recycled Bottle Windsock

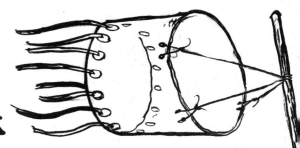

1. Clean and remove the label from a large plastic bottle.

2. Ask an adult to cut the top and bottom part off of the bottle (we are only using the middle part). At the top of the bottle punch 1 hole on one side and 1 hole on the other. At the bottom punch a hole every inch all the way around.

3. Take long pieces of ribbon and tie one to each hole at the bottom. Tie a single ribbon to both holes at the top to form a triangle.

4. Hang your weatherproof windsock on a pole or in a tree to see which way the wind is blowing.

Salt Dough

Salt dough is made from natural ingredients. You can use it like clay to make whatever you want, but don't eat it!

1. Mix 2 cups of flour, 1 cup of salt, and 1 cup of water. Make the dough whatever color you want by adding a few drops of food coloring.

2. Squish the dough into a ball. Sprinkle some flour on a cutting board and use a rolling pin to make the dough flat.

3. Break off small pieces and lay them down on a piece of wax paper to make flowers, bugs, people, or whatever you want.

4. Leave it in the sun for a couple of days until it is dry. Now you can make it more colorful by painting it!

Apron

Recycle an old T-shirt by turning it into an apron. All you need is a pair of scissors!

1. Find an old T-shirt and cut off the sleeves.

2. Make a cut all the way down the back of the shirt and open it up.

3. Now, cut a narrow strip up from the bottom of each side of the back piece and stop a few inches from the top.

4. Put on the apron and tie the narrow strips together behind your neck.

Dough Pot

1. Mix a small bowl of salt dough (see page 28).

2. Roll the dough into a long worm shape.

3. On a flat surface start making a coil with the dough to form the bottom of the pot. Then start to build up the sides by going round and round.

4. Leave it in the sun for a couple of days until it is dry. Then decorate your pot by painting it any colors you like.

Whistle

Here are instructions on how to make a whistle that you can keep in your pocket.

1. Carefully cut a small piece of paper to measure 1 inch wide by 4 inches long (you don't have to be exact).

2. Fold the 4 inch side in half and cut a small notch in the center of the fold about ¼ inch deep.

3. Fold the 2 edges down to the center fold so the paper becomes a small square.

4. Unfold the two edge pieces and place them up to your mouth using two fingers. Now blow air through the fold to make a whistle noise.

5. Keep trying, it takes practice to do it right.

Hacky Sackie

Hackie Sackie is a fun game that is played using only your feet. The goal is to see how long you can keep the ball in the air without using your hands, just your feet. Here's how to make your own ball.

1. Find an old sock.

2. Fill the toe of the sock with a small amount dry peas or beans to form a ball.

3. Cut off the rest of the sock. You only need the toe part.

4. Carefully sew the open end of the toe piece together.

5. Now go play Hackie Sackie!

Sock Puppets

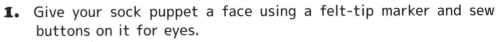

Rescue an old or unmatched sock from the garbage. Put it over your hand and now you have a puppet!

1. Give your sock puppet a face using a felt-tip marker and sew buttons on it for eyes.

2. Try making a dragon by pinching and sewing the back of your puppet into triangle shapes.

3. Use your imagination and make different types of sock puppets. Put on a puppet show for your friends and family!

Bunny Puppet

1. Find an 8½ by 11 inch piece of paper. Fold the 11 inch side into three sections.

2. Now fold the 8½ inch side in half. Then fold one side down to the fold, then fold the other side down to the fold. This will form a zig-zag shape.

3. Make ears out of paper and use a cotton balls for the eyes and the nose—add googly eyes to the cotton balls to make them more realistic. Draw whiskers on your bunny with a felt-tip marker. Put your hand inside the paper and you now have a bunny puppet!

Spinning Top

Make a top—a small *spinning* toy you can carry in your pocket.

1. Trace a circle on a piece of paper. You can use a small can to do this.

2. Color you circle using crayons, pencils, or felt-tip pens.

3. Carefully cut out your circle using scissors.

4. Find a pencil that is so short that you can't write with it. Push the pencil point through the middle of the circle.

5. Your top is now complete. Find a flat surface, pinch the pencil between your fingers and spin it. See how long you can make it spin.

Dried Fruit

A natural way to store fruit without using preservatives is to dry it. It's easy and fun to do.

1. Wash your apples, pears, or any other fruit, and dry them off using a clean towel.

2. Ask an adult to help you slice your fruit into thin pieces.

3. Next, using a needle and thread, make a string of fruit slices and hang it in a warm place to dry.

4. When it's dry and chewy, it is ready to eat!

> *Hot dry fruit drink: Put fruit into boiling water for 2 minutes, Turn down to lowest heat setting and simmer for 1 hour. It makes a nice warm fruity winter drink.*

Fruit Prints

1. Cut a fruit in half (you can also use a vegetable).

2. Place the cut side of the fruit onto an ink pad or some non-toxic paint.

3. Now, press the fruit onto a piece of paper to make a fruit print!

Popcorn
Christmas Decoration

Making things out of natural materials helps the earth. Here we can decorate the Christmas tree with popcorn garland and when Christmas is over, take the string off and put the popcorn outside for the birds and squirrels to eat!

1. Have an adult help you make some popcorn.

2. Take a needle and thread and make a few long strings of popcorn.

3. Carefully hang your popcorn garland on your tree for a natural decoration.

Snowflake

1. Make a square piece of paper by taking a corner and folding it down to the side edge forming a triangle. Cut off the excess paper at the bottom.

2. Fold the triangle over and over again to form a small wedge.

3. Cut off some paper at the bottom of the wedge. You can cut a notch, a half circle, or any other design.

4. Now, cut some designs into the sides of your wedge.

5. Unfold the paper and there is your snowflake! Hang it in a window using tape so you can see snow falling all winter.

Egg Carton Tulip

Instead of throwing away your used egg cartons, make some tulips out of them.

1. Cut out two egg holders from the carton and cut 4 notches around the tops of each piece to look like petals.

2. Place one egg holder inside the other one and using a pencil punch 2 small holes through the bottom.

3. Take a pipe cleaner and put it up through one hole and back out the other one and twist the ends of the pipe cleaner together to form the stem.

4. Make a leaf for your tulip by folding another pipe cleaner in half and wrapping it around the stem.

Newspaper Chain

1. Using scissors, cut a newspaper up into 1-inch wide strips.

2. Take 1 strip and tape the ends together to form a loop.

3. Next, take another strip of newspaper, put it through the loop you just made and tape those ends together.

4. Add more strips to make a long paper chain.

Easter Eggs

Coloring Easter eggs is so much fun. Here's a way to color your eggs by using natural ingredients like fruits and vegetables.

1. Have an adult help you put the eggs in a pot and cover them with water.

2. Add a teaspoon of vinegar and whatever natural dye you are using to the pot.

3. Simmer for 15 minutes and check the color. If the color is good, remove the eggs from the pot.

4. If you want a stronger color, remove the eggs from the pot and strain the liquid through a coffee filter into a bowl. Place the eggs back into the liquid and place the bowl in the refrigerator overnight.

Purple	....	Grape Juice
Violet	....	Red onion skin
Blue	....	Blueberries
Green	....	Spinach
Yellow	....	Lemon or peel
Brown	....	Black Coffee
Orange	......	Yellow onion skin
Pink	....	Cranberries or Beets

Pinecone Bird Feeder

1. Look for some large open pinecones that have fallen off the trees.

2. Put some peanut butter in a bowl and some bird seed in another bowl.

3. Roll the pinecone in the peanut butter, then roll it in the bird seed.

4. Tie a long string around it, hang it up outside, and watch the birds enjoy their new treat!

Milk Carton Bird Feeder

1. Find an empty milk carton and wash it out using soap and water.

2. Look for two sticks that are 2 inches longer than the width of your milk carton.

3. You will need to make 4 holes: 2 on the front and 2 on the back of the carton about a ½ inch up from the bottom equally spaced apart. Make sure the holes are a little smaller than your sticks.

4. Mark a small rectangle on the front and on the back ½ inch above the holes and a ½ inch in from the sides of the carton. Then cut the top and the sides of the rectangles and fold them half way down to form a V. Use scraps of cardboard and tape to make sides for the V.

5. Push the sticks through the holes from front to back so the birds have a place to stand.

6. Punch a small hole into the top of the carton and tie a string to it.

7. Fill your bird feeder with bird seed and hang it outside. Soon you will see many visitors come to your bird feeder.

8. To learn about the different types of birds, visit your local library.

Organic Glue

1. You will need a bowl, a ½ cup of flour, a sprinkle of salt, and some water.

2. Mix the flour and salt with the water, adding the water a little at a time. Be careful, you don't want the glue to be runny!

3. Use your new organic glue like any other glue when doing paper crafts. Make sure to give it enough time to dry.

Planet Earth Stained Glass

1. Tear colored tissue paper into small pieces.

2. Put a piece of wax paper on a flat surface. Using organic glue (see page 46), paste the pieces of tissue paper onto the wax paper in a circular shape to form the planet earth. Use other colors and sizes to make other planets.

3. After 24 hours the glue will be dry. Carefully peel the tissue paper off of the wax paper and hang it in a window just like stained glass!

Drawing Leaves

Trees serve many different purposes. They provide shelter for animals and help prevent erosion. Hickory trees are used for axe handles because it is a very hard wood, cedar lasts a long time and is used for fences, ash wood is light and strong and is perfect for making baseball bats. Sometimes its hard to tell what tree is what. An easy way to do this is by identifying the leaves. Drawing the leaf in a notebook is an easy way to remember the shape as you learn about trees.

1. Walk around your neighborhood or a park and collect different types of leaves.

2. Draw each type of leaf you find in a notebook. To learn about trees and leaves, visit your local library.

Bark Rubbing

Bark is the skin of a tree and is what protects the tree from harm.
Older trees have rough bark; younger trees are smoother.
Small trees make the best rubbings.

1. Find some old used crayons and peel off the paper.

2. Take a few sheets of paper and your crayons outside and look for trees.

3. Hold a piece of paper up to the bark and rub the crayon over it to get a mark that looks just like the bark.

Grasshopper Race

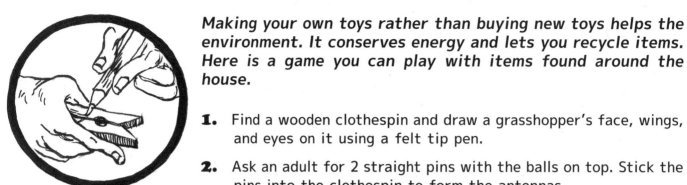

Making your own toys rather than buying new toys helps the environment. It conserves energy and lets you recycle items. Here is a game you can play with items found around the house.

1. Find a wooden clothespin and draw a grasshopper's face, wings, and eyes on it using a felt tip pen.

2. Ask an adult for 2 straight pins with the balls on top. Stick the pins into the clothespin to form the antennas.

3. Have a race against your friends and their grasshoppers. Press down on the clothespins and release them so they hop. The first one to cross the finish line wins!

Worms

Worms aerate the soil. This increases the amount of air and water found in the soil, which helps plants grow. Worms also break down organic matter and help fertilize the soil. One acre of land can have over one million worms in it.

1. Find a plastic container. Have an adult help you poke small holes around the bottom to drain water and a few holes in the top to let air in. The holes should be 1/8 inch wide.

2. Take a few scrap pieces of cardboard and paper and soak them in water. Lay the wet pieces down on the bottom of the container to make a bed for the worms.

3. Place some fruit and vegetable scraps on top of the bed, then add another layer of the wet cardboard scraps.

4. Add some worms to the container. Place the container on top of an old lid, big enough to catch any excess water from spilling over. In six months you will have rich soil that you can use in your garden.

Bugs on Sticks

Eating sweet snacks loaded with sugar are not very healthy. Here's a snack that is healthy, delicious, and fun to make!

1. Spread some peanut butter on a celery stick.

2. Sprinkle some granola onto the peanut butter. Place 2 raisins on top of the granola for the eyes.

3. Enjoy your tasty treat!

Bees

Bees are known for making honey. But the most important job they have is transferring pollen from plant to plant (pollination). If plants aren't pollinated, there won't be any new plants.

1. You will need a yellow and a black pipe cleaner and a pencil. Wrap the pipe cleaners around the pencil at the same time, then slide them off the pencil.

2. Make a small section at the end of the black pipe cleaner straight for the tail. For the face glue some googly eyes onto the other end. Now you have your own bee!

Box Dollhouse

1. Find 2 large boxes to recycle into a dollhouse.

2. Ask an adult to help you with the cutting. Cut two sides off one of the boxes and place it on top of the other box to form a triangular-shaped roof.

3. Draw windows and a door on the front of the box. Cut them out leaving one side attached so they can open and close.

4. Cut another door in the back of the house so you can put your dolls and toys inside.

Box Theater

1. Take a large box and draw a line 2 inches in around the edge of one side. Then make a line down the center.

2. You will need an adult to help you with the cutting. Make a cut down the center line then cut the top and bottom edges.

3. You just made two doors! Open the doors so people can see inside the theater.

4. Mark and cut 2 inches in around the entire bottom of the box. Now you have a hole to put your puppets through.

5. Find a table and put a sheet over it. Then place your box on top of the table with the back portion over the edge. Hide under the table and put your puppets up into the box. Now you can put on a puppet show for your family and friends!

Pretty Shoe Box

Don't throw out those old shoe boxes! Use them to store jewelry, toys, and other items.

1. Carefully cut up colored paper into different shapes.

2. Mix up some organic glue (see page 46).

3. Glue the colored paper onto your shoe box. Be creative and invent your own design!

Braids

There are so many different ways to wear braids. You can have a few braids, one big braid, or braids all over your head. Here are instructions on how to make a braid.

1. Divide the hair into 3 equal parts.

2. Holding all 3 pieces, take the left piece and put it over the middle piece. This piece is now the middle piece.

3. Now put the right piece over the middle piece.

4. Repeat this until you get to the end. Use a ribbon or an elastic band to end your braid.

Sundial

The earth and the other planets move around the sun like the moving parts of a clock. The earth takes exactly one day to spin around the north pole, and one year to travel around the sun. A sundial uses this movement to tell time by using the shadows made by the sun.

1. Using a compass, make a circle a few inches wide on a piece of cardboard (The size of the sundial is not that important.) Then, carefully cut it out.

2. Find the center point of the circle. Using a ruler, draw a line through it to divide the circle in half. Then, using a protractor, divide the circle in half again making four equal sections. Insert your compass into the center and draw a circle a little smaller than your sundial. Write N, S, E, and W inside the small circle.

3. Position your sundial so the N is facing north. Now it's time to start marking your sundial! At exactly 12 noon position your sundial so the shadow lines up exactly with the N. Now mark a 12 on the sundial.

4. Continue marking your sundial at hourly intervals. After you are done, you will be able to tell time without a watch!

The North Star

The North Star, also called Polaris, looks like a very bright star in the sky. Years ago sailors used to use the North Star to see what direction they were going when at sea. Here is how to find the North Star so you won't get lost.

1. Go outside on a clear night when you can see all the stars in the sky. It's best to do this in an area where there are no street lights.

2. Wait until your eyes get used to the dark. It can take up to 20 minutes for your eyes to adjust.

3. Find the Big Dipper. Look for the 2 stars on the far side of the cup. They will point up to the North Star.

Solar Powered Oven

A *solar-powered oven can reach a temperature up to 275 degrees. You can actually cook without using electricity. The only power this oven needs comes from the sun.*

1. You can use a cardboard box or a pizza box for your oven.

2. Mark a square 1 inch in from the edge on the top of the box. Have an adult help you cut the front and two sides of your square. Leave the back piece attached.

3. Fold up the flap and hold it in place with a pipe cleaner or a straw and some tape. Cover this piece with tinfoil to reflect the light into the box.

4. To keep the heat inside, cover the opening with plastic wrap.

Index